ULTIMATE GAMER

CAREER MODE

THE COMPLETE GUIDE TO STARTING A CAREER IN GAMING

THE AUTHOR WOULD LIKE TO THANK PETE O'SHEA AND ANDREW STEWART FOR THEIR HELP IN THE CREATION OF THIS BOOK.

KINGFISHER
LONDON & NEW YORK

Copyright © Macmillan Publishers International Ltd. 2021
Published in the United States by Kingfisher,
120 Broadway, New York, NY 10271
Kingfisher is a division of Macmillan Children's Books, London
All rights reserved.

Distributed in the U.S. and Canada by Macmillan, 120 Broadway, New York, NY 10271

Library of Congress Cataloging-in-Publication data has been applied for.

Author: Craig Steele
Illustrator: Berat Pekmezci

ISBN: 978-0-7534-7636-9

Kingfisher books are available for special promotions and premiums. For details contact:
Special Markets Department, Macmillan, 120 Broadway, New York, NY 10271.

Printed in China
9 8 7 6 5 4 3 2 1
1TR/1120/WKT/UG/128MA

ULTIMATE GAMER
CAREER MODE

THE COMPLETE GUIDE TO STARTING A CAREER IN GAMING

KINGFISHER

LONDON & NEW YORK

CONTENTS

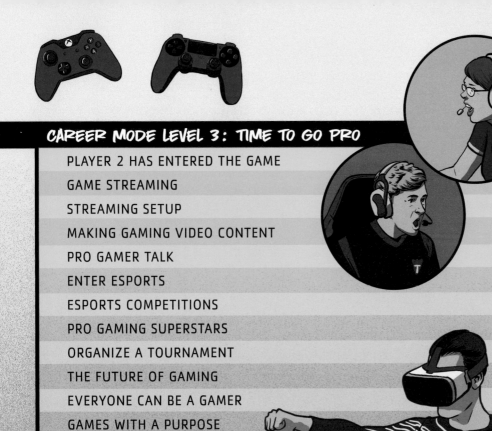

CAREER MODE LEVEL 3: TIME TO GO PRO

BIOGRAPHIES

Berat Pekmezci

Berat was born and grew up in Istanbul where he went on to study graphic arts. He first discovered video games with an X-Men arcade game in the mid-'90s and is still a big fan of 16-bit fighting games. With a keen interest in telling stories, he published his first graphic novels in Turkey. After working as an art director in advertising agencies for several years, he moved to London and has been illustrating books and cell phone games ever since.

Craig Steele

Craig is a computer programmer, gadget geek, and lifelong gamer from Glasgow, Scotland. He first started gaming on a Sinclair ZX Spectrum +2A and even loved programming his own games for it, too! Since then, he's survived a zombie-infested mansion in Resident Evil and topped the leaderboard in Dance Dance Revolution. Nowadays he's still a massive gaming fan and teaches interaction design and computer programming. He also runs workshops at Insomnia and Resonate Total Gaming festivals, showing people how to make their own games.

INTRODUCTION

Have you ever been told "it's only a game"? Well, if you're reading this book then you know it's so much more than that. As a gamer, you know it's about the thrill of finally solving the puzzle you've been stuck on, the fun of customizing your character the way you want, and it's about bravely going into battle with your friends. There's more to gaming than most people think, and there might be more to it than you think, too!

This book is about taking your gaming skills to the next level by playing career mode. Here you'll learn about the gaming industry and all the different jobs that are needed to build the games we love to play. From game designers and sound designers to coders and testers, you'll learn about how games are made from the initial idea to release day in stores, and the range of roles involved in making it all happen.

Building games isn't the only career in gaming today. There are new and exciting jobs where you can play games for a living—how cool is that? Today, streamers show their skills to the world on exciting livestreams and upload videos of hints, tips, and reviews for gaming fans to enjoy. And don't forget the competitive world of esports where professional gamers train hard to play for prizes on the world stage.

In career mode you'll learn that being the ultimate gamer isn't just about sitting in front of a console—you'll need to work on your skills if you want a job in gaming. These jobs aren't just for "techies" and there's more to pro gaming than mashing buttons. So if you think you've got what it takes to master career mode, read on and find out where your gaming expertise could take you!

A BRIEF HISTORY OF GAMING

Gaming hasn't always been the way we know it today. From humble beginnings to modern-day masterpieces, here's how gaming has changed the world over the last 50 years.

1970s

Atari launch a home version of Pong, a table tennis arcade game. It is one of the very first video games.

LATE '70s AND EARLY '80s

Space Invaders and Pac-Man arcade machines are hits, and most gaming takes place in huge arcades.

LATE '80s

The Nintendo Game Boy is launched—a pocket-sized gaming device that changes handheld gaming forever.

EARLY 2000s

Valve releases Steam—a service that allows games to be updated (and eventually purchased) over the internet, changing the way the world buys games.

. . . and Microsoft's first games console, Xbox, is released in 2002.

The Sony PlayStation is released in 1994 . . .

Home gaming consoles get a whole new look.

A speedy blue hedgehog named Sonic makes his debut. He'll later become one of the bestselling video-game franchises ever.

EARLY '90s

MID-'90s

2003

Online play becomes more popular through the growth of Xbox Live, PlayStation Network, and massive multiplayer online (MMO) games.

2009

With the rise of smartphones, cell phone games increases in popularity with fun hits like Angry Birds and Cut the Rope.

2010

Microsoft invents the Kinect controller, a new way to play games that uses cameras to turn your whole body into a controller.

2016

Also in 2011, Mojang releases Minecraft, a multiplayer survival game that would become the bestselling game of all time.

New game tech is being developed all the time, but Pokémon Go really puts augmented reality on the map.

2019

Twitch streaming site is launched. It is a dedicated platform for livestreaming games.

2011

League of Legends esports final is held in Paris, France. 15,000 people attend in person and 100 million viewers watch online.

FORTNITE

CAREER MODE
LEVEL 1:
LEARN
THE BASICS

GAME GENRES

So many games, but where to begin? To work in the gaming industry, you need to be clued in to all the games out there. There isn't just one kind of game—there are several, and whether you want something fast and action-packed or a brain-testing challenge, this is your ultimate guide to each genre of game and what they're about.

Super Mario

Adventure

Adventure games are about controlling a hero and going on a quest. These games are broken down into levels or stages that are set in different locations and increase in difficulty as you play along. As you progress, the main character destroys enemies, collects items, and learns new skills to become stronger.

Tomb Raider

Adventure games have brought us some of the most recognizable characters in gaming history!

Ms Pac-Man

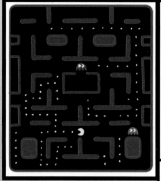

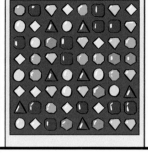

Candy Crush Saga

DID YOU KNOW?
The late '70s to mid–'80s is thought to be the golden age of arcade games.

Space Invaders

Arcade

These are colorful games with bright graphics and loud sound effects. The simple designs mean anyone can start playing without having to learn complex moves or rules. They have limited controls, often just a joystick and two buttons, and games like this are still made today as they're fun and easy to play.

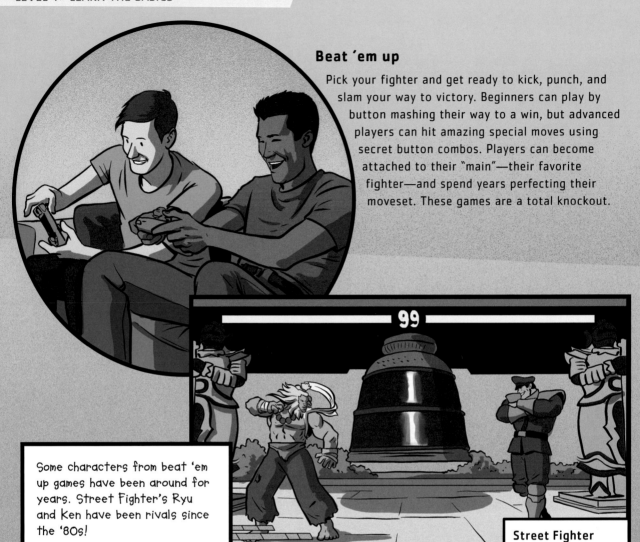

Beat 'em up

Pick your fighter and get ready to kick, punch, and slam your way to victory. Beginners can play by button mashing their way to a win, but advanced players can hit amazing special moves using secret button combos. Players can become attached to their "main"—their favorite fighter—and spend years perfecting their moveset. These games are a total knockout.

Some characters from beat 'em up games have been around for years. Street Fighter's Ryu and Ken have been rivals since the '80s!

Street Fighter

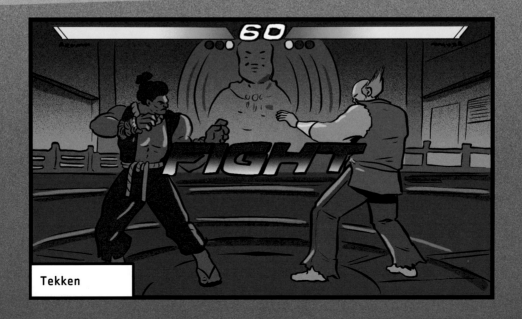

Tekken

Educational

Who said learning can't be fun? These games are both entertaining and educational. Whether it's learning how to touch-type accurately or practicing spelling or math, gaming is a stealthy way to develop new skills and knowledge. Players of the best educational games may not even realize they are learning at all!

Mavis Beacon Teaches Typing

Sumdog

Puzzle

These games are more about making your brain work rather than your thumbs. Puzzle games might have you fitting pieces together in the right order, or make you unscramble a pile of letters into a recognizable word. Rather than a health bar, these games might give you a time limit or restrict the number of moves you can make each turn. These addictive games make players desperate to "try again" until they solve it!

Tetris

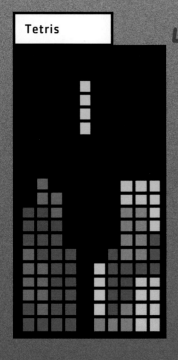

2 Dots

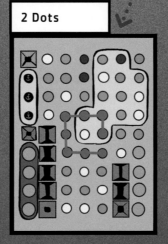

Crossword

Racing

Get behind the wheel of your favorite car or hit warp speed in an intergalactic spaceship. In these games, players can speed around a selection of tracks, navigating tight turns, steep slopes, and oil spills. Games like this keep players coming back again and again to improve their lap times.

Forza

Wipeout

Crazy Taxi

Some racing games focus on realism, recreating famous cars and race tracks in great detail. Others, like Mario Kart and Wipeout, are based in completely fictional worlds.

Call of Duty

Shooter

Blast your opponent in this fast-paced game genre. Many of these games place you in "first-person view"—you see the game world through the eyes of your character. To do well at these games, gamers need to be speedy and accurate at targeting and have quick reaction times. Players take on opponents across different maps that have hiding places and vantage points to make each game challenging.

Overwatch

WATCH OUT!
All games have an age rating, so make sure you only play games that are appropriate for your age.

Splatoon

Cities: Skylines

Simulation

Ever wanted to control your own world and make all the decisions? Simulation games put you in charge of everything—you can try out your dream job or control an entire game world. See what it's like to be the mayor of a cash-strapped city, or try to keep your zoo profitable while clearing up the elephant dung. The possibilities are endless.

Farming Simulator

FIFA 20

Sports

Football, basketball, skateboarding, and golf are all sports that have been turned into hugely successful video games. You can recreate a dream match with all your favorite players. Sports personalities change every year, so many of these games have annual releases to stay current.

Some sports stars claim that playing these games has improved their real–life performances, as they can practice new tactics in the game.

Madden 20

Age of Empires

Command and Conquer

Strategy

Players must plan their moves and out-think their opponent to win these games. Strategy games let players build an army or command an ancient civilization. Items and resources are limited, so each move needs to be considered carefully. Sometimes these games are "turn-based," meaning players make one move at a time.

GAMING GEAR

What players choose to play on is just as important as the game itself. Each device offers a unique gaming experience and also has its pros and cons. You need to get familiar with these bits of tech if you want to work in the gaming industry.

High-spec gaming computers

Gamers spend lots of time and money assembling and upgrading these dedicated gaming machines. As well as being powerful enough to play the latest titles, gaming rigs need to look good too!

Plug-in games consoles

These boxes are ready to plug into your TV and start playing. Consoles like the Playstation and Xbox are household names in gaming and are the top choice for a lot of gamers.

Portable games consoles

These are slightly less powerful versions of plug-in consoles that you can take on the move. Nintendo has a long history of making these machines, from the Game Boy to the Switch.

Mobile games devices

Mobile gaming on smartphones and tablets is a huge market and means games can reach more people than ever before. You no longer need a separate device to play the latest games.

High precision mouse

This is a mouse with gaming-specific capabilities, such as extra buttons and adjustable sensitivity. Turn the sensitivity up and you'll need less movement to move the cursor across the screen, which could be the difference between a character's life and death!

Game pads

These iconic controllers are a gamer's main form of input. Modern controllers feature over a dozen buttons, sensors, lights, and even speakers and microphones, and are tough enough to withstand a rage quit.

Wearable tech

Games companies are experimenting with more ways for people to interact with games. Virtual reality headsets let you play games in 360 degrees and soon we might see controllers that measure your heart rate and sweat levels (eww!).

Game-streaming box

Don't sit waiting for a download—these boxes let gamers stream games instantly, but you'll need fast internet speeds to take advantage of this latest tech. At last you won't need to worry about putting the disc back in the case.

Mechanical gaming keyboard

These high-performance keyboards let gamers feel every button press and their quick response time is great for fast-paced action. They're durable too, which is great for button mashers.

DID YOU KNOW?
Some games can only be played on one type of device. This affects what gaming machine a gamer might buy.

Speakers

High-quality speakers allow players to hear every detailed sound. Adjust the volume until it's just right—too much noise makes it difficult to spot crucial softer sound effects like enemy footsteps.

Gaming chair

These luxurious chairs give lumbar (back) support, keeping your spine in a good position. Adjustable arm rests and well-padded seats mean you can make yourself comfortable.

A fast network

Slow and laggy connections kill your chances of a high score. Use an ethernet cable to connect to the internet for a faster, more reliable connection than Wi-Fi.

THE PERFECT GAMING SETUP

Gaming isn't just about what's on screen—for the best gaming experience, a gamer's environment needs to be optimized too. Taking steps to create the best setup can improve gamers' comfort and focus, and ensure games run as smoothly as possible.

TOP TIP!
The best gaming equipment isn't always the most expensive. There are lots of articles online that compare equipment, so make sure to do your research.

CAREER MODE

LEVEL 2:

WORK IN THE INDUSTRY

THE LIFE OF A GAME

Before there were games, there were game makers—the people who create, design, put together, and sell our favorite games. From the initial idea to release day in stores, so many different people work on making a game what it is. This timeline shows the typical life of a game, and in the next pages you'll learn about each different stage and many of the jobs involved in making a game.

> **DID YOU KNOW?**
> Big budget games made by large game studios are known as "Triple-A" or "AAA" games.

How long does it take to make a game?

The life of a game can be very long—games with huge budgets produced by large game studios are made in many stages and take about three years to make. Luckily, some games take less time to produce. For example a small team of developers might speedily put together a prototype in a weekend and release the full game a few months later.

Brainstorm a new idea for a game
Month 0–3

It all starts with an idea for a new game. This is where the creative team kicks off the whole process and an idea gets approved.

Plan and design the game
Month 3–6

The next step is making sure the game's story, visual style, and sound design are mapped out by different designers, ready for building.

Sometimes games get lost in "development hell"—this is when they get stuck at a point in the process and can't move on. It may be because crucial staff have left the project or due to the company running out of money to make the game.

First-person shooter Duke Nukem Forever was announced in 1997, but spent so long in development hell that it wasn't released until 2011!

Release the game
Month 24–36

It's time to launch the game! Finally gamers get to play it, and game makers hope their hard work will be the next big hit!

Test the game
Month 24–36

This is the final chance for testers to spot and fix bugs and make sure the game is ready for people to play.

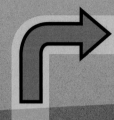

Build the game
Month 6–24

This is the stage where game makers create all the different parts they previously mapped out and developers assemble the game.

Market the game
Month 6–24

This happens at the same time the game is being made. The marketing team gets gamers excited about buying the game by planning advertising and events to shout about how good the game will be.

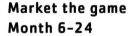

29

SPARKING AN IDEA

All games start as a simple idea. In a games company, everyone is responsible for thinking up new ideas for games, but it's up to the creative team to take these ideas further and refine them into what will eventually be the final game.

Any ideas for the game rules?

How about setting some time limits?

How do games get off the ground?

Many game companies have a creative director—a person who is ultimately in charge of which games get made. The creative director listens to ideas generated by their team and weighs up the positives and negatives of each one.

How about a game set underwater?

One of the goals could be to collect items for a submarine.

An idea might be approved because it's like nothing ever seen before—it could be a chance to create a totally new game. However, that is risky—a company could be spending a lot of time and money on a game that might flop. Other times, an idea might get the go-ahead because it's similar to another successful game. This is less risky because that style of game is already popular. The creative team needs to balance coming up with new ideas with understanding the trends of the industry and the types of games people are playing.

Mash-ups

Here's a way to invent new game ideas. Pick three items from the lists below and then mash them together to create a brand new game idea.

Settings

 Underwater

 Deep space

 A castle

 A futuristic city

 An island

Goals

 Collect all items

 Smash objects

 Solve the puzzle

 Defeat all enemies

 Escape

Genres

 Puzzle

 Adventure

 Arcade

 Strategy

 Educational

 Racing

 Simulation

 Beat 'em up

 Shooter

 Sport

Rules

 Don't touch the floor

 Can only use three items

 You can only go forward

 Time limit

Mash-up one

+

+

Ghost hunter Veronica Violet must find and capture all the ghosts wandering the halls of spooky Murdoch Castle.

Mash-up two

+

+

The player must repair the life-support system on a space station by connecting different pipes in the correct order. They've only got 30 seconds before the oxygen runs out.

GAME JAMS

Not all ideas are sparked in board rooms of big gaming companies. Sometimes they happen when gamers get together for a "game jam." This is an event where game enthusiasts team up and create ideas for future games. It's a chance for individual game makers to collaborate with other creative people to try to make the next big game release.

How game jams work

First, a team is formed. The best teams have a mix of talents and skills so each teammate can bring their own unique knowledge to the idea.

Then, the team checks the brief. Most game jams have a theme that the games must connect to. This keeps people focused and gets their brains buzzing with ideas.

Now the teams get to work and come up with cool ideas. There's limited time, so often they'll work late into the night. It's important teams get enough food, drink, and rest when taking part in a game jam.

Finally, game jams finish with teams presenting their ideas to the other participants. Most teams will have made a playable prototype or created some striking sample artwork.

Success stories

Here are some breakout games that started off as ideas created at a game jam.

Goat Simulator is a game where you get to play as a goat. It went on to make over $12 million in sales.

Home Improvisation lets you build flat-pack furniture and was a social media hit. It was streamed over 13 million times on YouTube.

After everything is wrapped up, teams might decide to continue working on the game idea because they think it's something special. It's fine if it doesn't work out because they still had a great time making it.

33

MAKING A MOOD BOARD

After coming up with an idea for a game, a team of game designers begin to bring it to life. To do this, designers will create a mood board that pulls together images, textures, and pictures of what the game world and characters might look and feel like. A mood board can inspire new ideas and helps the game makers understand the overall style the designers envision for the game. Check out what's on this mood board showing how designers bring together their ideas.

Mood boards can use images, text, photos, or videos—whatever works best to get the look and feel of the game across.

Rough sketches hand-drawn by designers can show off ideas for potential characters.

Many games have text as well as images, and designers might include a list of fonts they'd like to use on a mood board.

Designers often use photos of real-life places as inspiration for in-game buildings and locations. This is really useful for games set in real-life locations.

Designers will often create a color palette, which is a set of specific colors they will use throughout the game. Colors can affect the feel of the game—gray colors could make a game feel moody and bright colors can make a game feel zany.

Tear-outs from comics or magazines that match the designer's desired style are great pieces of inspiration.

Sometimes designers even take screenshots from other games that have a similar theme or style to the game they are creating.

VISUAL STYLES

A hugely important part of a game is the way it looks, and it's the job of the design team to create a visual style that suits the game's characters and story. Here are some popular visual styles used in video games that designers might choose from when making a new game.

Pixel art

Originally, game designers were limited to using just a few colors and pixels to create game art. However, many games still use this simple and quirky style. It might look basic, but it takes a lot of skill to create memorable game graphics using this approach.

Isometric 3D

This art style is used to create a 3D environment, usually as if you were looking at it from a fixed angle. It's often used in simulation games and role-playing games (RPGs) like The Sims, Age of Empires, and Two Point Hospital.

Abstract

Some games aren't based on the real world, or on anything at all. This art style is hard to pin down, but it carefully combines shapes and colors to create everything the player needs to play the game.

Photorealism

Some games try to create a world that looks true to life. Art directors working on action and adventure games use this style to create stunning environments and detailed, lifelike characters. The action in the game feels cinematic and draws players into the story.

Exaggeration

This design approach creates memorable characters that are larger than life—that's to say they're out of proportion compared to real humans. Big heads, huge muscles, or skinny legs can create cartoon-like art—like the characters from Fortnite Battle Royale.

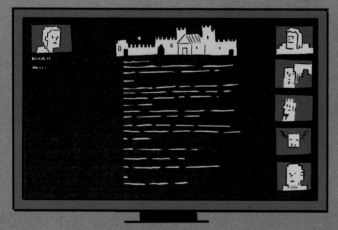

Text-based

In some games, the design is in the way that words are presented on the screen. By choosing the right fonts, colors, and thinking about the best size and position of the text, words on a screen can create a memorable adventure.

BEAT CHARTS

Once the idea for a game is mapped out on a mood board, game designers create the game's storyline. To do this, they use a beat chart, which is a visual design tool that shows the player's experience as they play through the game. This helps designers plot out a game's main milestones from the start to the ending.

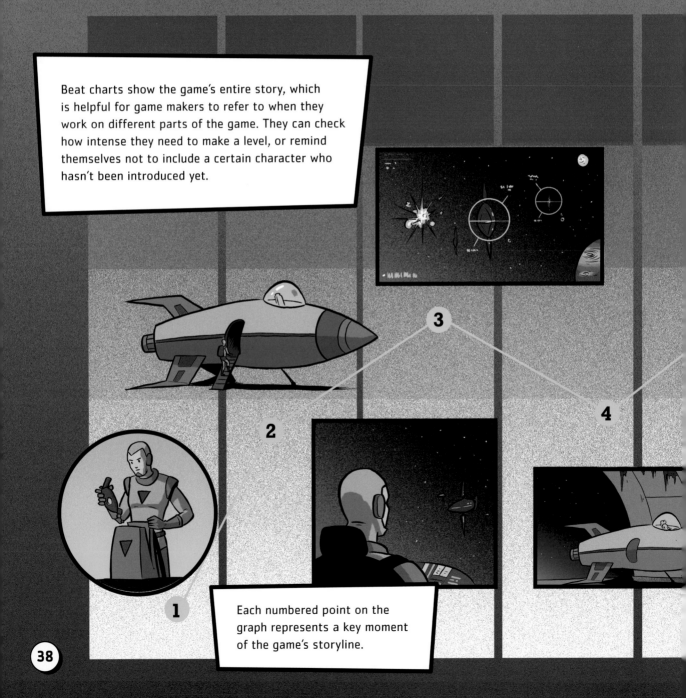

Beat charts show the game's entire story, which is helpful for game makers to refer to when they work on different parts of the game. They can check how intense they need to make a level, or remind themselves not to include a certain character who hasn't been introduced yet.

Each numbered point on the graph represents a key moment of the game's storyline.

Here is a beat chart for an alien adventure game. It shows the game's difficulty on the vertical axis and the duration of the game on the horizontal axis. Each colored column represents a different level. Many games start with easier stages then get more challenging as the game goes on. On this beat chart you can see how the game starts easy, then peaks in difficulty at the end where the player battles the final boss.

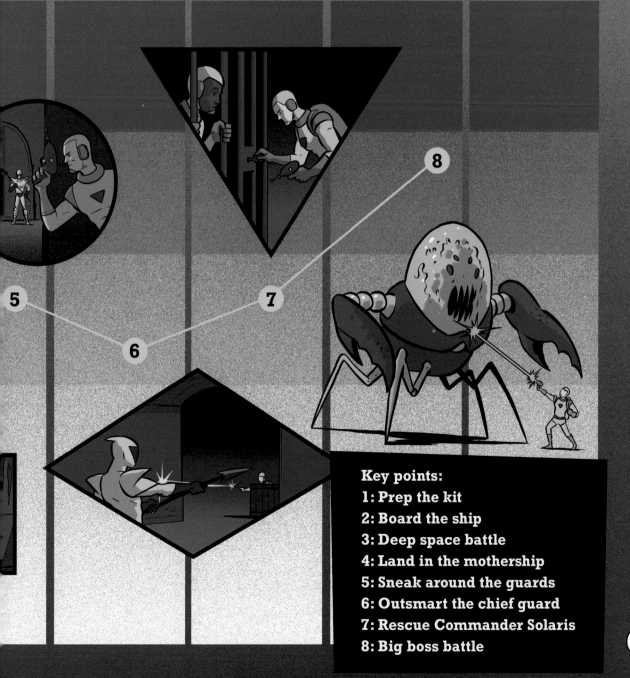

Key points:
1: Prep the kit
2: Board the ship
3: Deep space battle
4: Land in the mothership
5: Sneak around the guards
6: Outsmart the chief guard
7: Rescue Commander Solaris
8: Big boss battle

DESIGNING LEVELS

After the big features of the game are mapped out, the next task is to design the individual levels. Game designers use storyboards to plan the way players progress through each stage. They can show how characters move through a level, interact with objects, and reach their goals.

Designing storyboards

A storyboard looks a bit like a comic book—the panels are positioned in sequence and show the order of how the level is played. Storyboards typically start as rough sketches on paper. Even big game companies begin by hand-drawing their storyboards. By playing through the game on paper, game makers can spot big problems with the game's entire story or small problems with individual stages. It's much better to find mistakes at this stage rather than realizing after the game has been programmed and animated.

Level checklist

When drawing a storyboard, designers make sure it shows these three things:

1. The playable characters

2. Any special objects or collectables

3. How the player can interact with objects or move around the level.

Choose your path

Here are some examples of storyboards to show you how a designer can map out a level. This storyboard shows how the player, a knight, might solve a puzzle:

Each panel shows a different stage of the puzzle. The drawings are simple, but they make it clear what is happening, and sometimes captions are used to help explain the action.

This is a different type of storyboard. It shows two different paths the player might take to cross the level.

This is a single panel but it still tells the story of how the player might choose to play.

The green path is easier and avoids the enemy and pitfalls. The red path is more dangerous, but it rewards the player by letting them pick up gold.

When designing a game for a mobile device like a smartphone or tablet, game designers make their storyboard panel the shape of the device's screen.

GAME AUDIO AND SOUND DESIGN

Sound plays a big part in the way we experience games, and each noise you hear is recorded and mixed by a sound designer—from the sound made when you pick up items, to firing weapons and even selecting an option from the menu.

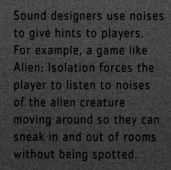

Sound designers compose and record the soundtrack for the game—the music that is played during each stage or level. They work alongside game designers to make sure their sound choices match the overall style of the game.

Well-designed sound can make a game feel more immersive. The sound design for a racing game like Forza Horizon is important, as creating realistic engine and driving noises draws the player into the game world.

Sound designers use noises to give hints to players. For example, a game like Alien: Isolation forces the player to listen to noises of the alien creature moving around so they can sneak in and out of rooms without being spotted.

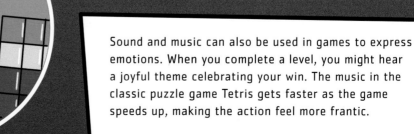

Sound and music can also be used in games to express emotions. When you complete a level, you might hear a joyful theme celebrating your win. The music in the classic puzzle game Tetris gets faster as the game speeds up, making the action feel more frantic.

Tools of the trade

Sound libraries

When choosing sounds for a game, a sound designer might record the effects themselves, or find them in an existing sound library. These are databases filled with sound effects that have already been created and can be used in any game.

Sound-testing tools

Specialist tools such as Audiokinetic Wwise let sound designers test their designs. They use these tools to plug different sounds and effects into a game, getting an idea of how it will work when playing.

Sound libraries aren't just for professionals. Check out page 63 to find sound libraries you can use to add music to games you make yourself.

PUTTING THE GAME TOGETHER

Now that the story, visual components and sounds have been designed, it's time to bring them together—that's where game developers come in. These are the people who write the code that brings the game to life. Without them and their digital skills, the games would just be ideas.

Get it together

The main role of game developers is to bring together all the game's assets (the graphics, 3D models, and sounds) and program the logic of the game. This means they write the code that controls how these parts work together, making the game interactive.

A developer might code the main character, the artificial intelligence that controls the enemy or even the user interface that lets players choose from menus or select items. They write the code that makes a car accelerate when the player pushes the X button and the code that controls the rival racer chasing the player around the track.

Key skills

Game developers have a specific set of skills that make them good at what they do. These skills are crucial for coding games.

Logical thinking Writing game code is all about understanding the rules of the game, then programming the game world to follow those rules. Developers must make sure every action they program makes sense to the game.

Attention to detail Absolutely everything in the game world needs to behave according to the rules, so it's important for game developers to write code that covers every possible situation that the player might try.

Pattern matching Many games share similar mechanics, meaning games of the same genre tend to be played similarly. Racing games usually use the same buttons to accelerate and brake. Game developers can spot these similar patterns. Knowing when to reuse code saves lots of time and makes it easier for players to play new games because it's like something they've played before.

Teamwork

It's rare for a game to be made by one person. Usually a big team of developers work together to build different parts. Some developers might be responsible for writing the code for an entire level and others might code just one small cut-scene.

Developers also work with other teams to make sure the game is built properly. Early in the process the developers will use placeholder images and graphics while the more detailed assets are being created by the game designers—this lets them build playable prototypes of the game and get feedback from the testing team.

DEVELOPER HARDWARE

Once the separate parts of the game have been created, it's time for the game developers to bring the assets (the visual elements and sounds) together. To put games together, developers use some of the most powerful tech around, and for big game studios, no expense is spared—their machines have the highest specifications.

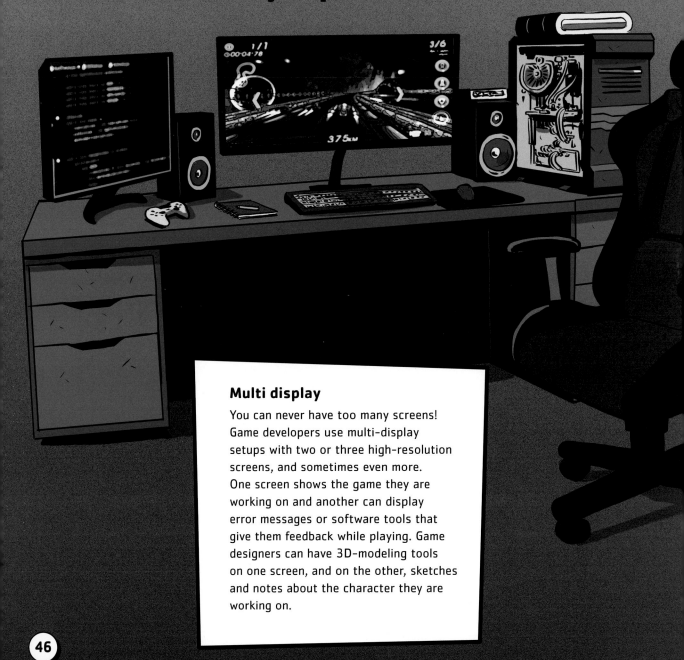

Multi display

You can never have too many screens! Game developers use multi-display setups with two or three high-resolution screens, and sometimes even more. One screen shows the game they are working on and another can display error messages or software tools that give them feedback while playing. Game designers can have 3D-modeling tools on one screen, and on the other, sketches and notes about the character they are working on.

Super-charged servers

Powerful servers are used to render games, which means turning the designer's 2D creations into 3D models or animations. Server rooms are packed with powerful computers that run 24 hours a day. These rooms get so hot they use cooling systems to prevent the computers from overheating.

Studio monitors

Studio monitors are a special type of speaker that play the game's audio as accurately as possible. At home you might choose a big pair of headphones or surround-sound speakers, but when making the game, developers need to ensure that the sound effects sound great no matter what type of speakers or headphones the gamer is using.

Powerful graphics cards

Game developers machines are packed with powerful graphics cards. This makes for a smoother experience when building and testing games, as high-quality images take lots of energy to run. These dedicated graphics cards can be expensive but it's worth it if they save developers' time.

Mega storage

Game studios have massive storage requirements— just think of all the audio, video, and 3D models they need to store for each game. They need to keep backups of every single game asset, which requires some serious storage space.

Game development kits

Game development kits (GDKs) are special versions of games consoles, like PlayStations and Xboxes, that make it easier to build games for different platforms. These machines cost about ten times the normal price of the console.

The development kits don't look like the actual consoles (sometimes they're just black boxes), but they come with special extras. For example, more USB ports or the ability to easily add or remove extra hard drives. They also have some features that are useful for developers, like status lights or a display screen that can show helpful error messages.

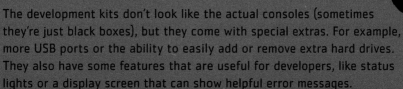

START YOUR GAME ENGINES

Game engines are specialist software used to power games. They come with tools that make developers' jobs easier and less time consuming. By bundling together common mechanics that are needed in every game, developers don't have to rebuild these features from scratch every single time.

Graphics engine

The graphics engine is responsible for drawing computer graphics and animations in the game. It is used to add and remove objects on screen at the correct time. For example, when a blaster is fired the graphics engine must draw the laser blast at the right position at the right time and make sure it's moving in the right direction.

Audio engine

The audio engine deals with the in-game sound effects and music. It makes sure the sounds are played (or "cued") at the right time, and makes sure they are mixed together to create the atmosphere the sound designer intended.

Physics engine

This is used to create the rules that determine how objects move and collide in a game. This could be how a tennis ball would travel when it's smashed with a racket in a sports game, or how a spaceship might move when it is being pulled into a black hole.

Artificial intelligence (AI) engine

This engine controls characters' or enemies' behavior in a game. A good AI engine makes a game challenging and fun to play, whereas poor AI results in a game that is too easy or impossibly frustrating.

Networking features

These features make it easier to create multiplayer games that can be played via a local network or the internet. They also allow developers to add features to games, such as in-game chats or trades.

Popular game engines

Engine: Unreal Engine
Developer: Epic Games
First released: 1998
Games made with Unreal Engine:
Fortnite Battle Royale, Life is Strange, Borderlands 3

Engine: Unity
Developer: Unity Technologies
First released: 2005
Games made with Unity: Mario Kart Tour,
Beat Saber, RollerCoaster Tycoon World

Engine: Solar2D
Developer: Corona Labs Inc.
First released: 2009
Games made with Solar2D: Zip Zap, Draw Rider, The Lost City

GAME TESTING

Before a game is released it needs to be checked and tested—this is the job of the game testers. Testing is a crucial stage of a game's life as it's the final check to make sure there are no technical problems (called "glitches" or "bugs") that would affect the gameplay.

The sound effects aren't playing on this phone. I'll add that to the report.

Game testers have a great eye for detail. They note any bugs they find while playing a game and compile them into a test report which they pass to the game developers to fix. The more bugs they can find before a game is released, the better the quality of the final game. Testers need to make sure the game works on every device it's available to play on.

Testing is usually carried out in two stages. Alpha testing comes first—these are tests carried out by staff from the gaming company. The second stage is beta testing, where gamers from outside the company are given early access to the game.

During alpha testing, copies of the game being tested are kept securely and are not allowed outside the testing labs. This is to help prevent spoilers being leaked to fans or rivals. The beta testing phase is usually the first look at a game for people outside of the game company.

Lucky gamers who are invited to play early versions of the game really help the testing process. Game testers check that players understand how to play the game, and by watching how they explore the levels and solve puzzles, they can judge whether the game is being played the way the designers intended.

TOP TIP!
If you make your own game, have some friends test it for you to help you improve it.

PROMOTING AND SELLING A GAME

It's the marketing team's job to get people excited about the game and encourage them to buy it, and their work begins long before release day. The best marketer understands what makes a game stand out to gamers, and with enough hype, gamers will pre-order copies or even line up to be the first to get their hands on it.

Get that promo

Marketers want to get news about the game out there to those who might buy it. For Triple-A games aimed at big audiences, this might include massive billboards, flashy TV ads or exciting launch parties. For a game aimed at a very specific audience, the marketing team may put on a small special event—for example, giving out limited-editon stickers or collectible figures.

Press preview

Once the game is announced, marketers handle requests from bloggers, vloggers, and journalists who want to publish stories about the game. Often, marketers organize special previews of the game while it's still being made, allowing bloggers and journalists to give their fans a first look at the upcoming game. The more people talking about the game, the better!

Overhyped

One danger with marketing is if the final game turns out to be different from what the advertisers promised. If this happens, gamers can be left disappointed and they might lose trust in the game studios. They won't want to buy their games in the future, which is why marketers need to know the game well and not make any false claims.

Making it in marketing

Would you make a good game marketer? If you can grab people's attention and convince people to try a new game, you could be a sales superstar. What's your favorite game? Try thinking of a way you would advertise it to your friends, and see how many you can make want to play it.

BUILDING A COMMUNITY

The life of a game doesn't end on release day. Many games are so popular that they form a community around them—a network of fans who really care about the game, its stories, and its characters. It's the job of the game community manager to listen to and support players and feed their feelings back to the game makers.

Community managers help build relationships with game fans by organizing online events, competitions to win merchandise, or chatting to players about what they enjoy about the game. This is because they want to create a community that players want to be a part of.

Community managers are also there to support fans with their queries. They'll help players by responding to issues or problems they're having with the game. This is an important job, as solving problems quickly will keep gamers happy and will make them want to continue playing the game.

Game community managers also gather insight into how players are playing. They'll look at gameplay information on data dashboards and use it to answer questions such as how long players are playing for on average, which is the most popular weapon or item, and even why certain levels take players longer to complete.

Reaching out to the community

Asking gamers to give feedback is a great way to understand how the community feels. Imagine a new feature is added to a first-person shooter game that lets players jump higher—game community managers will ask players what impact that new feature has had on their experience of the game: does it make the game more fun, or are gamers abusing this powerful new feature to win? This feedback can determine whether features or settings are adjusted in the next update.

Key skills

Relationship building—you need to be good at listening to and understanding people's concerns.

Experience—it's good to have experience of taking part in or running community events. Maybe you've been a team captain before.

Speak their language—you need to be comfortable talking about gaming so you can understand what issues players are having.

EXTENDING THE GAME LIFECYCLE

Even after a game is released, game makers may still be working on it. Sometimes they create new and exciting downloadable content (DLC) designed to extend the lifespan of the game and keep us playing it again and again. Game developers may plan this bonus content from the beginning, but other times it's in response to feedback from players.

Expansions

New levels, bonus characters, and additional storylines are great ways to expand the world of a game. These extras can develop the stories and characters of the original game in greater detail, appealing to fans. Once you've purchased an expansion pack, you can keep playing it for as long as you want.

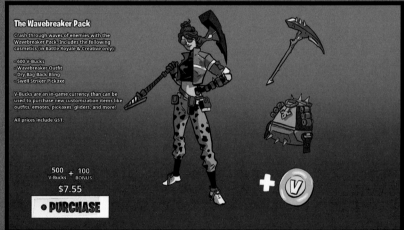

The Wavebreaker Pack

Crash through waves of enemies with the Wavebreaker Pack. Includes the following cosmetics (in Battle Royale & Creative only):

- 600 V-Bucks
- Wavebreaker Outfit
- Dry Bag Back Bling
- Swell Striker Pickaxe

V-Bucks are an in-game currency than can be used to purchase new customization items like outfits, emotes, pickaxes, gliders, and more!

All prices include GST.

500 V-Bucks + 100 BONUS

$7.55

● PURCHASE

Add-ons

Game developers sometimes give players the option to buy add-ons to help improve their playing experience—for example, extra "skins" (costumes) for characters, or items and abilities that were not made available originally. You should always get permission from the person who pays the bills before downloading any add-ons.

AVAILABLE NOW

ANGEL QTY'S MOST WANTED

LIVE FIRE

COLONY REBORN

○ ALL DLC MAPS, MODES, WEAPONS AND CLASSES A
○ NOT LISTED ABOVE: STEADY UPDATES OF COSMETI

Mods

Sometimes players or communities create their own modifications or "mods" for a game. This is usually outside the control of the original game makers. Sometimes mods can be small tweaks or changes, like changing a character's color, but other times they are deliberately destructive. For example, some players create mods to "hack" the game by letting them cheat against other players.

WATCH OUT!
Remember that mods are made by fans, not the original game company—so be careful before downloading any mods from the internet. Always check the reviews to see if they have a good rating.

Nerf

Have you ever played a game where a particular item is overpowered compared to others? It can be really unfair to players who don't have that item. Game developers sometimes step in to change the rules, making that item less powerful. Gamers would say that item has been "nerfed," meaning it's been changed to be much less effective. It's important that game developers make these changes to keep games fair and fun for everyone.

Expansions and add-ons are a big part of the gaming industry. Often, free-to-play games can only make money if players purchase these add-ons. Some people think that add-ons are fine if they only affect how characters look, but if you have to buy extras with real money to have an in-game advantage, it's not fair for everyone who plays.

TITANFALL 2

THE ROAD AHEAD

COMING SOON

MORE MAPS:
GLITCH, RELIC

NEW TITAN:
<<CLASSIFIED>>

NEW PRIMES:
RONIN & TONE

NEW LIVEFIRE MAPS:
TRAFFIC, DECK

MORE
FREE
CONTENT
TO COME
>>>

JDED FREE WITH TITANFALL 2.

THE VIDEO GAMES INDUSTRY

Step back and look at the bigger picture. All the different jobs in gaming are connected to each other, creating the wider gaming industry. The people in these roles work together to make the games we play a reality, and each person's different role is valuable to get the game from being just a cool idea to the final product in the player's hands.

Developers

You've met this bunch—they're the people or studios that make the games. Whilst a game is being built, developers will look for publishers to take on their game and release it to consumers.

Developers > Publishers >

Publishers

Publishers are companies that handle the business aspects of releasing games. They're in charge of making games available for people to purchase, the marketing and promotion of games and deciding how much games should be sold for. EA, Sony and Nintendo are all examples of publishers.

Retailers

Retailers sell the game. This could be a physical shop, such as a supermarket, or an online app store such as Steam Store.

Consumers

Consumers are the gamers who buy and play the games—that means you!

Not every game follows this chain. Sometimes developers sell their game directly to consumers using crowdfunding. They raise money by asking fans to make small donations to fund building the game, and once it's made, fans who contributed receive a copy of the game. Crowdfunded games feel more personal to fans.

Publishers mostly work with game developers outside of their company, but sometimes they make games "in house." This means their own staff build the game. In this instance, the publisher is also the developer!

Publishers can be retailers, too. For example, the Apple Arcade service lets gamers play a mixture of games, and Apple collects the subscription payment from those customers. Here, Apple not only makes the games available to consumers, but also sells games to consumers.

Some big companies get involved at every stage. Sony Interactive Entertainment has is own team of developers who make games. Sony are also the maker of PlayStation, so it may publish its own games specifically for PlayStation consoles. It also acts as a retailer and sells its games directly to consumers through the online PlayStation Store.

Retailers   >   Consumers

Exclusivity deal

Sometimes a publisher might make a deal with developers so that a new game will only be available for their consoles. If it's a popular game this may drive more people to buy their console. However, this type of deal might upset gamers who don't have that console.

GAME MAKERS HALL OF FAME

These super-talented game makers have all earned a place in the Hall of Fame. They've used their creativity, digital skills, and artistic talents to make their mark on the gaming industry.

Hideo Kojima

Will Wright

Hideo Kojima is a game director who is most well known for creating action and adventure games including the Metal Gear Solid series and Death Stranding. Hideo likes being involved in all aspects of making a game, and is often the lead writer and designer on his projects. He runs his own independent game studio, Kojima Productions, in Shinagawa City, Japan.

Will Wright is a game designer who specializes in making simulation games. Starting with the city-building game SimCity in 1989, he went on to create a series of popular and influential games including The Sims and Spore. Will believes that games are a great way to help teach people and argues that games can help prepare us for the complex world we live in.

Jennifer Hale

Shigeru Miyamoto

Jennifer Hale is a talented voice actress who has played a whole host of video-game characters. Jennifer plays Ashe in Overwatch and Commander Shepard in Mass Effect, as well as various appearances in games like Mortal Kombat 11, Halo 5, BioShock Infinite, Call of Duty, and multiple Star Wars games. She holds the world record as the most prolific video-game voice actress, having appeared in over 160 games.

Shigeru Miyamoto has designed some of the most iconic characters in gaming. He is the creator of Mario, Luigi, Donkey Kong, and Link. He started as a student developer making arcade games for Nintendo and went on to to create the second bestselling video game series of all time: Mario. The Mario series has sold over 400 million games worldwide. He is now the Creative Fellow of Nintendo.

Kim Swift

Kim Swift is a game designer who led the team that made the award-winning puzzle game Portal. The idea started as a small student project which was then spotted by the game developer company Valve who hired her to make it. Kim also designed the zombie-survival game Left 4 Dead and the epic Star Wars Battlefront II.

TOP TIP!
If you want a spot on this impressive wall, check out the next page on how to make your own games.

DO-IT-YOURSELF GAMING

You don't have to be a professional to make an awesome game. There are lots of tools to help you design and build games on your own. Check out this list of tools recommended by gaming-industry pros—they're simple enough to use, but powerful enough to make exciting and engaging games.

Game making

Construct

www.construct.net
Construct is a great app for making 2D games. You don't need to know how to code, instead you can quickly create games using "drag and drop" blocks that put the code together. Even better, the games you make using Construct can be published on Steam, the Apple App Store, and Google Play Store.

Pygame

www.pygame.org
Pygame is a set of coding tools specifically made for building games. It uses Python, one of the most popular computer programming languages in the world. Pygame gives you access to sound libraries and special graphics to use in games. New to coding? Search for Pygame Zero for an even easier way in.

GameMaker Studio

www.yoyogames.com
This tool lets you create several different types of games—everything from role-playing adventures to racing games. You can even export the games to play on consoles including Nintendo Switch, PlayStation 4, or Xbox One. It's available to try out for free.

Graphics

OpenGameArt.org

opengameart.org
OpenGameArt.org hosts a huge collection of game art available to use in your games for free. You can find images to use as characters, backgrounds, and objects in your game. Using top-quality art will make your creations look and feel more professional.

Blender

www.blender.org
Blender is a free tool for creating 3D models. You can create 3D models and characters for games, animated films, motion graphics, or even design objects to print with a 3D printer.

Audio

Freesound

freesound.org
Freesound has a massive library of sound effects. It has lots of different beeps, bloops, and loopable music that's perfect for a game soundtrack.

Unity Asset Store

assetstore.unity.com
The Unity Asset Store has a bunch of free sounds, ambient sounds, and music. These are high-quality sound effects that are used in many professional games.

Smartphone recording

Every smartphone has an app that lets you record sound and the mics in these devices nowadays are pretty good, too. Go out and record the world around you and you might capture some interesting noises that could fit in your game in an unexpected way.

You can download all these tools for free, but make sure you get permission from whoever owns the computer—otherwise it might be Game Over!

CAREER MODE
LEVEL 3:
TIME TO GO PRO

PLAYER 2 HAS ENTERED THE GAME

Part of the fun of gaming is playing with friends. It's not often you get to take on a zombie apocalypse with your pals, but gaming lets you do that. In recent years, people have made new gaming careers that focus on this social side of gaming—streaming is all about playing games with an interactive audience. But multiplayer mode came long before streamers . . .

Gaming arcades

Video games have always been a social experience. Gamers would hang around arcades, feeding the machines with their pocket money. Although the games might seem simple compared to today's blockbusters, there was pride in cheering on your pals and being good enough to get a top score, earning your name a spot on the leaderboard. Even today's games use online leaderboards, letting gamers boast about their wins.

Couch play

When game consoles arrived, multiplayer gaming turned into "couch play"—where you'd sit beside someone and play a game at home. Game companies had to find innovative ways to allow new multiplayer modes. Turn-based games relied on you passing the controller and split screens divided up the action when playing racing games. Some game makers even designed extra hardware like the PlayStation Multitap adaptor, which allowed up to eight people to plug in simultaneously. That's a lot of wires!

Modern gaming allows for massive multiplayer online games (MMOs).

DID YOU KNOW?
Game companies had been trying to develop online gaming since the '80s, creating consoles that could connect to each other using phone lines.

The space role-playing game EVE Online can handle over 60,000 players at the same time.

Going online

The early '90s saw multiplayer gaming take on a whole new look. Machines with ethernet capabilities allowed gamers to have Local Area Network or "LAN" parties by connecting their machines to the same place. Then in the early 2000s, game companies took advantage of improving internet speeds to launch online multiplayer games, meaning players could game together from their own homes.

New ways to play

Nowadays, we have more ways to share games than ever. There are online chat servers for talking with teammates and in-game trophies to unlock and post on social media. Some controllers even have "share" buttons built in, so you can upload gameplay for your friends to see with the touch of a button. Playing together truly is a fun and popular way to game, so it's no wonder multiplayer mode has led to new gaming careers.

GAME STREAMING

Today, the gaming industry isn't all about making games, it's about playing them, too. Professional game streaming is a new career where streamers make a living by creating gaming video content. By broadcasting live gameplay or recording it and uploading it later, streamers create an interactive viewing experience with an audience. Streaming may look simple, but in this line of work many things happen behind the screen.

Get on the platform

Streamers need places to host their shows, and websites such as Twitch and YouTube let gamers broadcast their gameplay to an online audience for free. The platforms make money by showing ads, and if a streamer is popular some of that advertising money will be shared with them. Fans may also choose to give money to streamers directly by making donations or paying for a subscription to their channel.

Sponsorships

Sponsorships are another way streamers can earn money. Streamers might be paid by a company to promote a game or gaming product. A company that designs gaming chairs might pay a famous streamer to showcase their product on the live stream, as it is a product the streamer's audience might be interested in. It's serious business, so streamers must be honest about which parts of their streams are paid for by sponsors.

Make some noise in the chat

The best part about streaming is the chat and conversations. The chat feature lets viewers send messages to the streamer and discuss the game with other viewers, making the viewing experience more personal. Some streamers even let viewers influence what they do next in the game, asking viewers questions like "Where shall I go next?" and "What character should I play as?". Great streamers connect with their audience, which keeps viewers coming back to watch more.

The left path has better items to use.

The punk girl has the best attack combos.

Words of advice

Here are a few tips streamers swear by to help them create the best gaming video content.

Set a schedule
Stream regularly and at the same time—that way people will know when you're likely to be online.

Pick a popular game
Streaming a game that everyone is talking about is a good way to attract viewers. But don't be afraid to stream more obscure or old titles—each game will have its own audience.

Engage
Ask viewers for their opinions on the game, and listen to what they say. You're more likely to get people subscribing if you care about your audience.

Thanks! Say thank you to people who subscribe or send gifts.

WATCH OUT!
You must be at least 13 years old to create your own channel on YouTube and Twitch. Until then, you could record videos just to show your friends and family.

Green screen

A green screen lets you change your background by using a chroma key effect to swap the green screen for an image or video. Chroma key effects are available in video editing and broadcast apps.

Key light

This illuminates the streamer's face so every expression can be seen clearly on stream.

High-quality microphone

Having good-quality sound is just as important as video. A good microphone placed at the right distance will pick up what the streamer says clearly.

Keyboard and mouse

An attractive keyboard and mouse look great on stream. Backlight keyboards and mice are popular choices for streamers.

Streaming deck

Pressing these buttons cues sound effects or on-screen animations—a fun touch to any stream.

High-resolution camera

Streamers make sure the lens is clean and pointing toward them at all times (sounds obvious, but people move around a lot when gaming and sometimes end up out of the shot).

STREAMING SETUP

Streamers spend time perfecting the setup of their room and streaming equipment to make sure their stream is visually entertaining and also run as smoothly as possible. The equipment they use is vital, but it doesn't need to be super expensive—it's all about putting it together in a way that makes the stream look slick and professional.

Multiple monitors

One screen is used to play the game and the other runs the software that broadcasts the gameplay to the internet.

Capture card

One end plugs into the console, the other into the computer. This sends the video output from a games console into the computer, allowing the streamer to record or stream the gameplay.

MAKING GAMING VIDEO CONTENT

There are two popular ways that streamers make and share gaming video content. Either they can record themselves playing a game to share later, called a "Let's Play" video, or they can broadcast themselves playing a game live, called a "live stream." Streamers use different techinques and software to create the different kinds of gaming video content.

How to make a Let's Play video

1. Make a plan
First, streamers pick a game and think about how they want to showcase it. They could play it all the way through, called a "run through," or play it using certain rules, for example limiting the amount of items they can use.

2. Write a script
Streamers then write some notes to remind them of the key points they want to cover in the video. They start with a fun introduction, then explain the challenge before playing the game. They always need to leave time to wrap up at the end and tell people where they can find their other videos.

3. Record the gameplay
Streamers use a screen-recording tool or a capture card to grab the video from their games console.

4. Edit the video
Streamers use video-editing software to trim parts of their recording so they only show the most exciting or important parts—no one wants to watch hours of irrelevant gameplay! Free software like Apple iMovie and OpenShot are great tools for editing.

5. Upload
Finally, they post their video to YouTube, Twitch, or other video sites where it's watched by followers and fans.

How to broadcast a live stream

1. Tool up

Lives treams are hosted on sites such as Twitch and YouTube, so before starting anything, streamers log into the platform they wish to stream on. Streamers also use special software to help them broadcast live, such as OBS Studio, and stream decks trigger commands, changing things up on screen.

2. Mix the visuals

Streamers use the broadcasting software to mix different visuals together. They combine live video from the game with video from their camera, alongside text and graphics. This is done before going live so that everything looks neat when they start the live stream.

3. Go live

Once they have their visuals in place, there's time for one last test and then 3, 2, 1 . . . time to go live. Streamers start playing and viewers in the chat start talking.

4. Cut it

Broadcasting software lets streamers cut between different "scenes" while they're live—these might be different camera angles, or other videos they've prepared. "Openers" are videos used at the start of streams and "stings" are transitions— usually graphics that show information quickly. Streamers might use a sting to introduce the Q&A part of their stream.

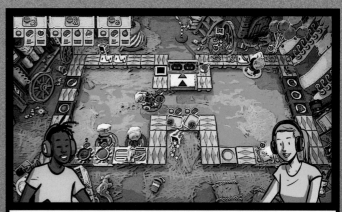

5. Special effects

To make their broadcast exciting, streamers sometimes add special effects. They might apply filters over everything to brighten up the video, or make fireworks or confetti appear when they finish a level.

PRO GAMER TALK

Can you talk the talk? Streamers often use game-specific language when commenting on their gameplay. They might talk about how long they spent grinding or what their favorite PvP game is. Get ahead by learning these common words and phrases used in online gaming.

MOBA

Stands for multiplayer online battle arena—a mode of play in strategy games. Players fight alongside teammates and are rewarded for playing well together and managing resources wisely.

Grinding

Doing the same task over and over again to earn points or gain items. For example, this might mean having to defeat 25 trolls before your character can progress.

Battle royale

A multiplayer mode where the aim is to be the last one standing—the final player left at the end of the game. Players try to survive as long as possible and must find supplies and weapons to help them outlast their opponents.

PvP

Short for player versus player—a one-on-one match with an opponent. PvP games have you go head-to-head with a friend or nemesis.

Pwned

If an opponent is completely defeated, they've been pwned. It's an in-joke among gamers based on a game designer mistyping the word owned.

MMORPG

Stands for massive multiplayer online role-playing game. These games feature thousands of players controlling characters and interacting with each other all at the same time.

Campers

Usually seen in multiplayer games, campers are players who stay in the same spot so they can easily pick off other players that pass by.

No scope

A trick-shot in shooter games where the player shoots their target without using the sights on their weapon.

Latency

The time it takes for commands to go back and forth from the computer to the game server, measured in milliseconds (ms). 50ms means it takes 50 milliseconds to exchange messages with the game server. The lower this number is, the less likely you'll notice any lag.

Noob

Players who are new to a game and unskilled are called "noobs" or newbies. The only way to get rid of this label is to get good quickly!

ENTER ESPORTS

Esports is short for "electronic sports." These are competitive gaming events where professional gamers take each other on in battles, competitions, and tournaments. Sometimes these competitions are online events streamed over the internet, but they also take place in real life in massive arenas with thousands of spectators.

ESPORTS COMPETITIONS

The best gamers in the world have turned their hobby into a job. Professional esports players make money by winning cash prizes in tournaments. They might also have sponsorship deals from companies that pay them to use their products or wear their merchandise while they compete. Only the very best players can make gaming their only job.

Need to know

Tournament
Teams play against each other for a grand prize—beating another team knocks them out of the competition. Early rounds in tournaments may have hundreds of players.

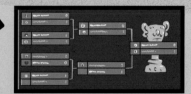

League
Competitions held over a long period of time, where teams play against each other multiple times. Teams' final positions are decided by their wins and losses across all matches they've played.

Leaderboard
A board that shows the scores of competitors in order of best to worst. In gaming, the first leaderboards came in arcade games where "high scores" were listed alongside gamers' names, showing off how good those players were.

Popular esports games
These games have a reputation for being played professionally the most. Check out these stats to see just how popular they are.

League of Legends
- First released in 2009 by Riot Games
- Professional leagues around the world in North America, Europe, South Korea and Brazil
- The 2018 World Championship final was watched by 200 million viewers

EVE Online
- First released in 2003 by CCP Games
- Players build their own spaceships and take them into battle
- A massive online war that took place in 2014, called the "Battle of B-R5RB," involved over 7,500 players. The real-life cost of damages to their virtual ships was around $300,000, making it the most expensive battle to have taken part in at the time

Showcase events

Some esports tournaments are massive and have a viewership of over 10,000 people. Here are some mind-blowing stats about the biggest competitions.

The International
• First held in 2010
• Total prize money is over $25 million
• The biggest Dota 2 tournament in the world
• The final takes place in a huge arena in Shanghai, China with 18,000 spectators

Overwatch World Cup
• First held in 2016
• All teams taking part share the prize money equally
• Players team up to represent their country, not their normal esports team
• South Korea were champions in 2016, 2017, and 2018

PRO GAMING SUPERSTARS

The popularity of esports and streaming has sky rocketed, with professional gamers becoming as recognizable as athletes and film stars. It might seem like a new star is born overnight, but the most successful professional gamers and streamers have been working for years on their craft. To be the best in the industry, pro gamers train every day on strict schedules and streamers spend hours writing, filming, and editing their content for us to enjoy. Take a look at these famous gaming pros and their amazing achievements.

Gamer Name: Ninja
Real Name: Richard Tyler Blevins
Known For: Professional streamer and YouTuber
Top Game: Fortnite Battle Royale
Special Skill: Trains up to 12 hours a day
Random Fact: Reached one million subscribers in less than a week on former streaming platform Mixer

Gamer Name: Scarlett
Real Name: Sasha Hostyn
Known For: Professional gamer
Top Game: StarCraft II
Special Skill: First woman to win a major international StarCraft II tournament
Random Fact: A top-earning gamer with total winnings of over $357,000

Gamer Name: Pokimane
Real Name: Imane Anys
Known For: Professional streamer
Top Game: League of Legends
Special Skill: Speaks English, French, and Darija (Moroccan Arabic)
Random Fact: Has over four million subscribers on YouTube

Gamer Name: SumaiL
Real Name: Sumail Hassan
Known For: Professional gamer
Top Game: Dota 2
Special Skill: Is always 3 steps ahead and can predict attacks
Random Fact: At age 16 he became the youngest player to surpass $1,000,000 in earnings

Gamer Name: HelloKittyRicki
Real Name: Ricki Ortiz
Known For: Professional gamer
Top Game: Marvel vs. Capcom and Street Fighter
Special Skill: Esports veteran, having competed for over 20 years
Random Fact: Favorite fighting character is Chun-Li from Street Fighter

Gamer Name: N0tail
Real Name: Johan Sundstein
Known For: Professional gamer
Top Game: Dota 2
Special Skill: A master of strategic thinking
Random Fact: In 2019 he won the International Dota 2 Championship, earning over $3,000,000

ORGANIZE A TOURNAMENT

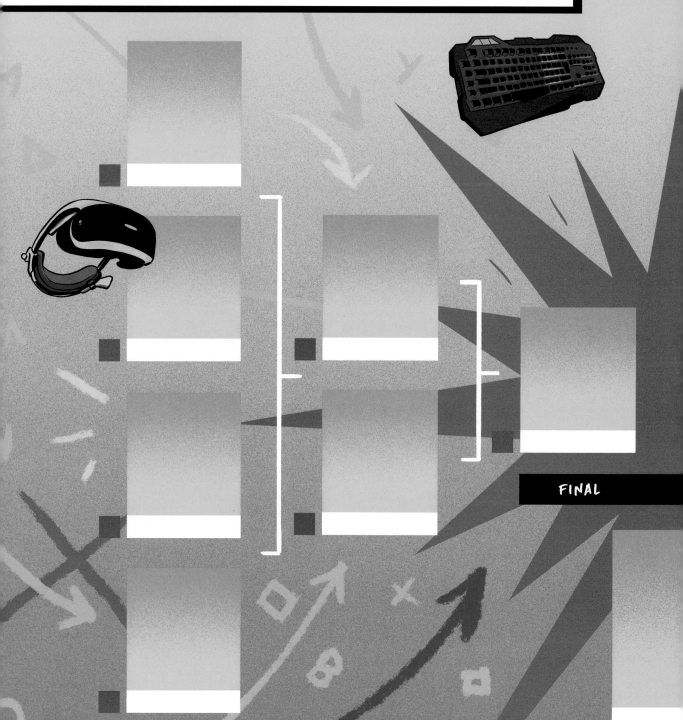

FINAL

QUARTER FINAL   SEMI FINAL

Taking part in leagues and tournaments is a great way to boost your profile as a competitive gamer. Now's your chance to organize your own tournament and see who will be crowned the Ultimate Gamer Champion.

For this tournament you'll need eight players and your favorite multiplayer game. The first round should be made up of four pairs, with four winners advancing to the next round. Two winners from the second round will then advance to the final and battle it out to become the ultimate champion. Put each player's gamer name in the outermost boxes and fill in the remaining boxes with the winners of each round. Don't forget to snap a picture of this template to use again and again.

FINAL

SEMI FINAL

QUARTER FINAL

THE FUTURE OF GAMING

The gaming industry has progressed massively since the 1970s and is continuing to change all the time. What will we see over the next decade? There'll be new consoles and gaming gadgets more powerful than ever, worldwide hits that everyone will want to play, and obviously a few fails, too. What new careers will we see? Here are some predictions about the future of gaming...

A better balance

Games are for everyone regardless of their gender, and the number of women working in games is expected to rise over the next ten years. We will see more talented women break into the gaming industry and make their mark.

More games, more game makers

Building new games will be easier than ever. New, simple-to-use software will mean everyone could become a game maker, in the same way camera phones make it easy for anyone to share a snap. Expect to see more people making games than ever before.

Take control

How will we control the games of the future? Rather than a handheld controller, maybe a full bodysuit will make our bodies the controller and games will respond to our heart rate or breathing pattern. Imagine a haunted house game that gets scarier the more you sweat!

Better than the real thing

Improvements in sound and graphics will make games more immersive. Stunning sights and environments might tempt people to stay in the gaming world longer. We'll need to think about how that affects us as humans, balancing a perfect "digital world" with our imperfect real world.

Sporting future

As the popularity of esports soars, these events will become bigger and better. Maybe we'll see esports at the Olympic Games? Future esports champions need to start training now in preparation for the world stage.

85

EVERYONE CAN BE A GAMER

Nowadays there's no such thing as a stereotypical "gamer." Unlike in the past, you don't need to own a console or powerful PC to get into gaming, you can simply pick up a smartphone and go. And that's not the only way gaming has changed to include everyone. Check out some of the ways gaming has improved to become more accessible to each kind of player.

Today we have more games than ever that suit a range of ages, from infants and teenagers to adults and even older players. Different generations can play the same game, meaning more fun for everyone.

Look, we can choose different skin colors for our characters!

Games also offer players more choices about who they play as. Instead of just one character with a fixed look, now you can build a character that better reflects you, meaning everyone can be the protagonist of their own game.

Games aren't just for boys game makers are designing games with everyone in mind. More women than men play mobile games every day.

New assistive technologies make it easier for everyone to play. Screen readers are used by people with visual impairments to speak out instructions and adapted controllers allow people who can't use their hands to play their favorite games.

Great shot, dude!

Lastly, game characters and stories are starting to reflect the world that we live in. Some games tell stories that are similar to the lives we live, with all kinds of situations and relationships. These advancements in games make people feel included, and we can expect to see more improvements in the future.

GAMES WITH A PURPOSE

While some games have you collecting treasure or running from zombies, others have an even greater purpose. These games can be used to help people solve problems, practice difficult tasks, and even save lives. Game makers have shown that games can not only be entertaining, but have a positive impact on the world. We can expect to see more games like this in the future.

Prepare for takeoff

Some simulator games are used to train pilots. It's much cheaper to let pilots practise on a computer than behind the controls of a multi-million-dollar airplane. These are similar to games you can play at home but with extra features that are designed to work with the high-tech simulator machines.

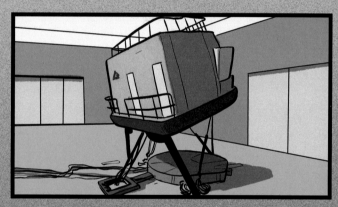

Medical training VR

Surgeons use the same VR technology as mainstream games to help them plan and prepare for difficult surgeries. They practice complex procedures as many times as they need to on a virtual patient before performing the surgery for real.

Genes in Space

This game was designed to help scientists better understand cancers. Each level is designed using a DNA pattern and gamers steer their rockets through the path to avoid asteroids. While playing, scientists collect data about which genes are faulty in cancer patients, which helps them identify these genes in real life.

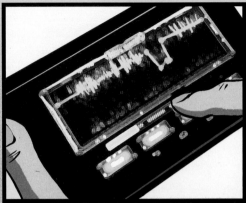

Chill out mode

Some games are designed to be relaxing, reducing anxiety and stress. Simple puzzles, soothing soundscapes, or playing around with colors are great ways to improve your mood and focus your thoughts.

Level up your mind

Who said learning can't be fun? Many games are designed to be educational. They can teach you how to touch type, help you prepare for a driving test, and even highlight health and safety hazards around the home.

BREAKING INTO THE GAMING WORLD

You've learned about the different jobs surrounding the games we love, so what next? Here are some suggestions to help you kick-start your own career in gaming. Get going and soon you could make the next big hit, have millions of viewers online, or be playing games on the world stage.

Get game making

If you feel like you've seen every kind of game out there and have an idea for something that's not been done before, it's probably time to design and build your own game. You can start by using the software mentioned on pages 62–63. Make sure you share the games you build with your friends, then you can see how fun they are and if they work well or not!

Team up

If going solo isn't your thing, look for gaming groups either online or in your local area that you can attend, with an adult's permission, of course. You'll meet other people who share an interest in playing and making games, and you could also recruit members for an esports team.

CoderDojo

Learn some skills

Try looking up school, college, or university courses that could be an option in the future. Courses in game development and design, coding, business, and marketing are a great way to learn valuable skills. Or you can learn without taking a course by using library books, industry magazines, and online tutorials to teach yourself exactly what to do.

Work experience

Maybe you want to work for the top dogs of the industry? Well you're in luck as some games companies will offer you the chance to visit their offices to work for them for a short period of time. This lets you see what it would be like to work as a game maker.

Create, share, get feedback

To improve your work, show it to someone and ask them for feedback. If you make a game, ask someone to tell you what parts they love and what parts they don't like, or if they found anything confusing. If you want to be a streamer, maybe record a video and show it to your friends, then ask them if they enjoyed it. This way you'll know exactly what you need to work on. Keep repeating this and your work will get better and better.

CHOOSE YOUR CAREER PATH

Are you a tech genius who's an ace at writing code, or are you competitive to the max and eager to play games at the top level? Follow this flow chart to see which job in the gaming industry you would be most suited to.

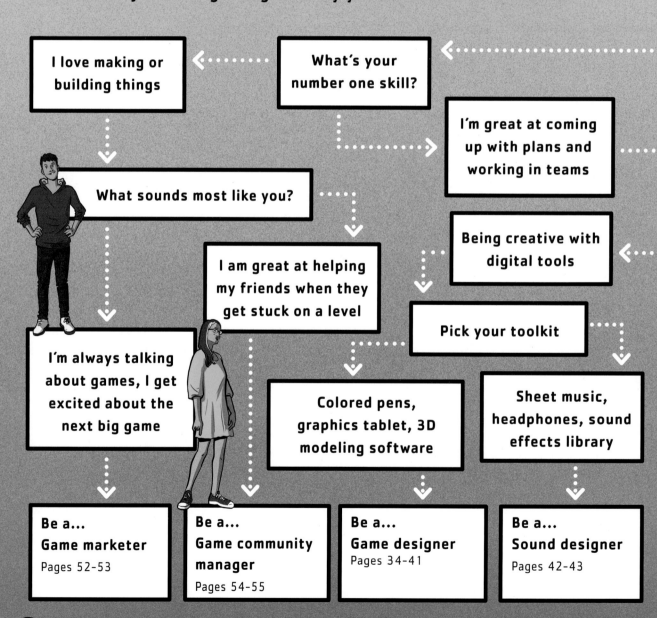

What's your number one skill?

I love making or building things

I'm great at coming up with plans and working in teams

Being creative with digital tools

What sounds most like you?

I am great at helping my friends when they get stuck on a level

Pick your toolkit

I'm always talking about games, I get excited about the next big game

Colored pens, graphics tablet, 3D modeling software

Sheet music, headphones, sound effects library

Be a...
Game marketer
Pages 52-53

Be a...
Game community manager
Pages 54-55

Be a...
Game designer
Pages 34-41

Be a...
Sound designer
Pages 42-43

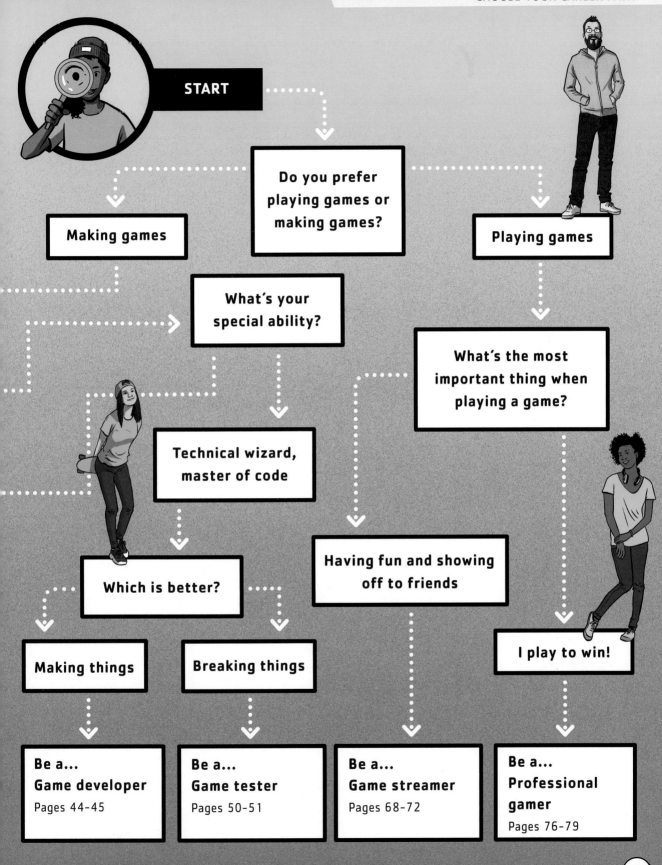

START

Do you prefer playing games or making games?

Making games

Playing games

What's your special ability?

What's the most important thing when playing a game?

Technical wizard, master of code

Having fun and showing off to friends

Which is better?

I play to win!

Making things

Breaking things

Be a...
Game developer
Pages 44-45

Be a...
Game tester
Pages 50-51

Be a...
Game streamer
Pages 68-72

Be a...
Professional gamer
Pages 76-79

93

GLOSSARY

alpha test The first stage of the game-testing process. These tests are carried out by the game developers and they look for bugs and glitches in the game.

audio The sound effects, music, and noises used in a game.

augmented reality A type of game that mixes graphics and sounds from a game with physical objects in the real world. Pokémon Go and Minecraft Earth are examples of augmented reality games.

beta test The secondary stage of the game-testing process. Gamers are asked to play and test a version of the game, so the game makers can find more bugs.

capture card A piece of hardware that lets you display the video output from a games console on your computer.

chroma key effect A visual effect that replaces a colored background of a video, such as a green screen, with another image or video. Streamers use this effect to layer the video of their gameplay on their streams.

downloadable content Also known as DLC, this is extra game material not included in the original game, such as levels or characters, that is available to download.

esports Sports competitions where professional gamers compete against each other playing video games, either as individual players or as a team.

ethernet A wired connection that connects a computer to a network. This connection is much faster than Wi-Fi.

game engine Software used by game makers to build and create games more easily. Game engines have tools that allow common features of games to be built quickly.

graphics The visual elements of a game, including images, text, environments, and 3D models.

hardware The physical parts of a computer or gaming setup.

Let's Play A type of gaming video content where gamers record themselves playing through a game with commentary on their experience.

live stream A live video broadcast online that viewers can watch and often interact with.

monitor An electronic screen used to display images. You can connect a monitor to a computer or games console to display video games.

role-playing game A type of game where the player plays as a character, and is responsible for their character's actions. The decisions they make throughout the game affect that character's abilities and overall story.

server A huge and powerful piece of computer hardware that can be used for many different purposes. A server may be used as a place to store and host an online game, or it may be used by a developer to store assets for a game that they are building.

software Programs that can be run on computers and gaming consoles that perform specific tasks, such as game engines or video-editing software.

sound library An online collection of pre-recorded sound effects and music available to be used in games.

specifications Often shortened to "specs," these are the details that describe a computer setup, such as the type of processor and how fast it is, and the amount of storage space, or computer memory.

stream deck A control panel with buttons that can be programmed to enable sound effects or on-screen animations for streamers to use during their live stream.

streamer Someone who makes gaming video content and posts it online, either as a Let's Play or as a live stream.

virtual reality Computer-generated images that are combined to create a fake environment that can be experienced through sights and sounds using special technology.

visuals Graphics, images, and animations that a streamer uses to make their live stream exciting to watch, such as a border or follower counter.

INDEX